Cracks in the Path
Brenda Goggs

Cracks in the Path
ISBN Paperback: 9781761099151
ISBN Ebook: 9781761099168
Copyright © text Brenda Goggs 2025

Cover image: Photo by Brenda Goggs
Design by Graham Davidson

First published 2025 by
GINNINDERRA PRESS
PO Box 2 Bentleigh 3204
ginninderrapress.com.au

Contents

The Botanical Gardens I	5
Danger Keep Out	6
The Botanical Gardens II	7
Carpaccio makes a movie	8
Curtin	10
Autumn's fire	11
Trade Goods	12
Flints	13
In December I wonder	14
Living the lie	15
The Arboretum	17
Summernats	18
The Superb Parrot	19
There and back	20
Welcome	21
Tumbleweed Town	22
West Basin	23
The little boy	25
City Plaza	26
Counsel for the Defence	27
Alpine Botany	28
Open Heath	29
If only	30
Airport	31
Sergeant Duncan Carseldine, POW, knits himself a jumper using fencing wire for needles	32
Australian War Memorial	33
When you are a teacher	34
Weston I	35
Weston II	36
It finally rained today	37

Oakey Hill Electricity Substation	38
The National Museum	39
Northbourne Avenue reborn	40
Autumn Elegy	41
Yesterday	42
Billboard Boasting	43
A cry of witnesses	44
Autumn	45
Gardeners	46
Canberra	47
Capital Hill trepanned	48
Bunnings I	49
Bunnings II	51
Bunnings III	52
On Lake Tuggeranong	53
At the Portrait Gallery	54
Civic Plaza	55
Clear Complexions	56
Eric Thake, War Artist, Noemfoor Island, 1945	57
Grave Dimensions	58
Storm in the Outback	60
Ngalyod the Rainbow Serpent	61
Ngayunangalku	62
At the Portrait Gallery	63
George Lambert, Self-portrait with Gladioli	64
Parliament House Democracy. Closed for Refurbishment	65
The Tram	67
The frost	68
Outreaches	69

The Botanical Gardens I

In the gardens, plants are labelled neatly,
not sown in rows, but artlessly displayed.
This little well-planned chaos subtly, sweetly
suggests a world's new Gods, nature betrayed.
Strange desert rocks bleed blood from purple veins,
trucked in, across three thousand miles or more.
Transplanted desert in the Canberra plains
look better yet after a fresh downpour.
To call it conservation justifies it
saves us a trip as we make it our own,
identity, exotic place to sit,
landscape, culture, belonging quickly grown.
So what you see is truly what you get
on our terms here, we've wind and wildness yet.

Danger Keep Out

Time meets life head on:
Across the brittle gum lawn
A tree has fallen.

The Botanical Gardens II

An English garden vaunts
some almost riotous excess –
A cherry tree whose blossoms dwarf a building
stands in an Oxford courtyard, overblown, celestial,
in spiritual bloom.
Fragile, outrageous,
a visible prayer, suspended, flutters.

Here in these antipodean rocks,
red rust, yellow ochre stain and crust,
jasper rime and acid crystal,
purple flowers in a bed of fire soil,
red and purple shadows lying silent,
a confession, nagging, yearns.
Unyielding, silent rocks of ages
whisper and stutter.

I ache and I sigh
I pray in the why.

Carpaccio makes a movie

Forget the Scuola Grande and their frescoes; I'll make a movie.
A study in epic, a story built on myth but equal to Rome.
Move the campanile aside so the palace can be viewed more easily,
polychrome and gilded, a cosmopolitan city glitters and beckons.
There is only one bridge over the Canal;
the Virgin is endlessly breached yet entire.
Behold the miracle of the possessed boy,
witness the Great Fire at the Doge's palace,
be stirred in the sleep of St Ursula visited by an angel.
Venice pretends to be Brittany,
St Jerome and the lion can pass through the desert
to the imaginary Port of Dover
and the Reception of the Ambassadors will still take place.

The audience has gathered, the present is everywhere.
The women are indoors overlooking the square
where the men stand, looking sidelong, comparing
their civitas, mediocritas, egalitas.
State Officers may wear red.
The young men who wear tights and are too young to govern
parade their potential.
It will all end in tears, but the canal will run gold,
the sunset a neap tide which laps time and limns decay.
The paying public, the mingling of clans in confraternities,
suburbanities, eternities, vanities,
cradle their purses bulging with popcorn and nuzzle
orbs of ice cream vaulted in chocolate.

Papers rustle like the latest on dit.
Important updates arrive on silent shivers to rattle handbags,
ruffle skirts and pulse in pockets
while they wait for the spectacle, over and over,
to make sense of the everyday.

Event Cinemas. Check session times for viewing near you.

Curtin

At night, the velvet darkness transmits wi fi,
wild and high fidelity across night space.
I hear the lions roaring at the zoo,
roaring because they roar and cannot remember why.
The distant sighs of cars on the parkway
signal ascent without gear changes.
It is uniformly late, too late for gears,
they just point and press into the darkness.
The possum rends the velvet dark with hiss and spit,
spites the roses whose beauty is on lay-by
and lurks because possums lurk, skulk and hide.
A line of hand-built wall on Cotter Road, like the blanket's edge
mutely holds the wakefulness of people in the night
protected from the noisy light of tomorrow,
delineates the scrap of bush between me
and the lions.
We swap a hollow roar of night.

Autumn's fire

Driving home from Magnet Mart a column of smoke
billowed into view
in the direction of my suburb, my house.
For a terrible moment I envisaged my pile of mulch, an eruption

in flagrante in the middle of the park, licking the autumn
leaves of the trees above,
an embarrassing hulk of body parts on display
because I was not there at the end,
for 'closure'.
The fallen tree has yielded but it is smoking underneath,
an angry wound, an inflammation swells.

Tree's revenge? The remnant of the heart still pulsing
after the amputation,
after the life support has been turned off
and the mulcher has been with his sickle's swath.
Ashes to ashes, dust to dust.
A haunting scent of pine in summer,
wisps of smoke on the cool, clear air
are quickly despatched for good with my shovel.
Danger averted.
It was someone else's fire, somewhere else.

Trade Goods

Relics from a forgotten land	Hand
Sculpted, hammered, carved from sand	Mind
Tiny planes of glass fracture	Capture
Leaves of flint create a picture	Rupture
Glinting light, pearlescent tint,	Flint
Serrated glances, iris print	Squint
Fragments of wine bottles flaking	Cracking
In each shard your heart is breaking	Quaking
My favourite museum relic chosen	Wizen
The air, the flight, the prey is frozen	Midden
Elegant tips of transparent spears	Sears
Hang, crystal shivers of unshed tears.	Fears

Flints

Grinding, rubbing two stones against each other
                    Land lease lapsed
Hammer dressing, gently tapping one stone against another
                    For your own good
Percussion flaking, striking one stone with another
                    Broken beer bottles
Pressure flaking, pressing against the edge to remove small flakes
                    Drinking the wine of regret
Working edges of tools are blunted, disembodied, taxonomied
                    Indigenous becomes a technical term.
Flints of glass decorate my wall.

In December I wonder

if I am not, after all, a plant.
Summer shade is a shallow bluff.
What promises made, where zephyrs play,
are only night thick.
By morning, all bets are off.
The gentle rehydrating, skin unfurling air
has turned to blisters by noon
and I am losing suppleness, my tensile core,
that 'green fuse which drives the flower'*
in a dew-kissed 'green and pleasant land',†
my chlorophyll joie de vivre, my shine.
Here I hang, waiting out the hours
till I fall for the promise of night again.
It will not last, but even the lie,
glaring, unremitting and blatant,
will be worth it for the while
till tomorrow, until March.

* Dylan Thomas, 'The Force That Through the Green Fuse Drives the Flower'
† William Blake, 'Jerusalem'

Living the lie

Waiting to have my hair coloured
I scan the four magazines
that are sitting here
and find four truths.

I ignore the offer of cellular water
and have a flat white to match my hair.
I stir it, observing the froth
that no longer catches the light.

Like my hair, no doubt,
it just stores calories
which silently slide down
to my stomach and hips.

I am early and they chide me gently,
no irony included: we all know
it is about lateness,
Better late than never.

Now I wait while they work,
we reconsider that friend's candid comment
that I 'took so well': My goodness!
I didn't recognise you, you look so much older.

They cluck and reassure.
Time tucks away trust and complicity
and I am still grey
although my inner self is young

and still quite new
at this time of the morning.
Then I have my bought hair on
and we can all relax.

Slow thinking is mindfulness
Slow food is fresh, whole and unadulterated
Slow craft is artisanal and alchemical
Slow fashion is hard wrought, bespoke, unique.

Slow aging requires a responsible approach.
I must do my bit for us all.

The Arboretum

Never, No, not ever,
The fascination of the bound foot,
Subtly crippling, breaking, bending, binding,
Restraining, wrapping, rewiring, lying.
Redesigning, re-engineering, rebuilding, re-creating
into tiptoe, poison precariousness, minute, elusive enchantment
born from tradition, culture, breeding, status,
and pain. Pain for beauty, pain in power, pain in process.
And yet I am smitten by bonsai. Call it pen jing
penzai, shumu, shuihan, suiseki,
Chinese and Japanese meet Latin with
a nomenclature of impunity.
But it is
the same.
While I
long to
protect,
to admire,
wonder,
and am
swept away
by their
beauty,
I am,
Deep
Down,
A hypocrite,
Looking for excuses, visiting them in autumn,
To hear their whispered secrets, their inaudible cries.

Summernats

'Summergnats',
revheads and their chicks
lurch along, bauble boobs burned and bursting,
words falling out of their mouths,
loud and raucous as cockies
as they perve and swerve,
plumes frisking.
Boys will be boys: their squires leer, jeer and joust,
flash their testosterone torsos or
flex their flab so their tattoos dance and quiver.
Walking past the hairdresser
they make kisses on the window
and offer themselves for a quickie
they can't afford and aren't likely to get.
The doors are locked.
The roar of engines, flash of virtual flames
and squint of chrome
attract other representatives of their species
and the great DNA swill is swapped.
Preening, idling, swarming,
they shimmy in clouds of bluster,
raunchy revving and alcohol fumes,
no smoke without fire, until they are burnt out
and it is all over till next year when the warm
tickles summernuts and they are in season again.

The Superb Parrot

leans into the blossoms,
shreds blooming in its beak,
like pieces of cloud.
It holds two twigs at once,
one in each claw
as it hip hops in the air.

The end of term is here
and I could be that shred
dangling in the beak of time,
where clouds of forms, reports and marking loom.
Too many conversations happen at once,
I am standing on two twigs moving apart.

I lean into the promise of
holidays.
Quiet.
Slowness.
The sound of birds.

There and back

There is a certain restraint in a city curve,
a suggestion of tension,
not truly letting go but 'gesturing'
with subtle control but concrete decision.

A 'dog's hind leg' is, therefore,
a critique of the curve, a dog of a curve,
insouciant, carefree,
a flagrant spring, arcing along.
Curved nose to the ground, it snuffles,
lurches off on each curved tangent
and lifts its leg
while its owner stands patiently or
forges a straight line through
the wagging tails on gridded paths.

But there is the curve on the road
to Belconnen where the broad sweep of an arm
of bitumen encompasses the heart and the urge for home
as it shuts out the valley and the horizon
to hold me in each return.

Welcome

Today at Norgrove Park in Kingston, ACT,
little Maryrose Aurelia Phoenix
was officially named and welcomed
into a community of chosen well wishers.
A slender phoenix from the ashes of
paid up barren disappointment,
Maero glows with promise.

But what of those other little birds,
grey and gawky, small and insignificant,
shy and full of startle,
whose fugitive appearance is too early,
too short and lost in migration,
fallen from the nest,
ousted by the cuckoo, clawed by eagles,
a few feathers fluttering earthwards
or fallen from an angel.

Parcel of hope,
an arm's warmth
holds the moment
against whatever the future will bring.

Tumbleweed Town

The harvest is completed,
Christmas hunger is saturated and wishes placated.
the Boxing Day sales have beseeched,
boasted and boxed treasures for
second breakfast, and
Christmas consolations.
Empty seedpods rattle,
purses exhale and suck in their cheeks
and banks withdraw behind ATMs,
hives focused inwards.
Sun parches January open and
Canberra Avenue is bleached empty.
Heading south of centre the suburbs fold in
on themselves and quiet descends.
The tumbleweed town reveals itself,
rind abandoned, clothes undone.
Parliament is in recess,
political staffers are at the coast,
businesses are closed till the 4th, the 9th,
the 27th, when Australia Day
shakes off the torpor, flexes muscles,
looks in the mirror, and after a self congratulatory
romantic smooch with its reflection,
the new year begins.

West Basin

The health giving benefits of a walk around the lake
A coffee from the booth
Are known. Fresh air, sun screened sparkle of light
kids on scooters, segways glide by
The ripple of water lapping subtly at the ankled shore
rowers cleave diamond water
Tamed and trained by beauty and townscape
A jewel setting for beautiful living
Refresh the jaded suburban soul.
The water jet shoots sky high,
Arcing perfection

The health giving benefits of exercise by the lake
64% wanted push ups
On new gym equipment are proclaimed.
60 chin ups, 40 body curls
A muscular display in sweaty sparkle,
step ups & sit ups 32,
The ripple of flesh and flab lapping subtly at the waisted shore
tricep dips 20
Tamed and trained by glamour and bodyscape hamstring
stretches,
Refresh the dimpled soul.   *Hamstrung by appearances,*
Watch us perfect ourselves

The health giving benefits of a walk together by the lake
We trade words
Are known. Fresh air, slow sparkle of conversation shared,
echo consoles echo
The ripple of tears and laughter lapping subtly at the crooked shore,

                                      we are silent together
Elbow to elbow,   *The carillon stands alone*
Linked by Friendship and friendscape
                            but no man is an island
Refresh the dented human soul.
                            We bridge the perfect gap
                            Inside out.

The little boy

is having his hair styled
at the stylist's.
A master of Korean cool stoops low
to trim his neck and the hair around his ears
while he gazes stolidly into the mirror,
his eyes small, guarded windows in the glass.
He sits while the style is created,
his hair blown in ruffles of handheld,
warm, wind-blown, caressing air
atop his small stillness.

Somewhere, aged 10 like him,
a girl is waiting for him in the future,
with the prospect of
microdermabrasion for $25,
half legs
with cosmetic injections,
forehead lines,
lip and chin,
frown lines or crow's feet,
wrinkle treatment,
open on Sundays.

City Plaza

Walking through the city
my shoe shop has gone
and giant grey billboards
have replaced it.
A svelte, alluring man
surveys the passers by,
suggestive, but his words are not his own.
On his right, a sophisticated, seductive female,
surveys the women wanting
him to speak to them.
Below, two doors
are cut into the wall, unobtrusive,
nearly invisible.
Here's possibility after all.
Is it in or is it out?
Here wordlessness has a future:
in the end, it's not about the eyes,
it's where you put your feet.

Counsel for the Defence

Did our forebears in dissipated times
have a monopoly on sin?
When justice was not only blind but
wore a domino to hide behind;
when women were always wrong,
when birth spoke louder than morals
and the poor were always untrustworthy
(some sins live long).
What new sins remain to lure,
seduce, to lapse into and languish beneath?
Leaning back on the sofa, cup in hand
as time ticks by,
the sun is shining after the fog has lifted,
winter leaves dance, cold fritillaries,
and warmth gleams, golden.
The day is reborn before your eyes
and, just for you,
the promise is made,
but you are watching TV at midday.

Alpine Botany

There is nothing here
except rocky outcrops,
silent granite witnesses
of time's passing.
The wind eddies and furls,
flutters and chivvies
loose bits of clothing
in wordless chatter.
I have left my city self behind
and I am here alone,
unwinding,
casting off layers and crusts.

My shadow looms ahead
and inside its dark contour
I am counting species
searching another crowd
for familiar faces,
recognition with delight.

The busy population
jostles, seethes, nestles, clings,
clutches, waits, stands, creeps and sprawls,
but in slow motion.
There is no destination here
for I have arrived.
The answer lies in the question:
beauty is infinite.

Open Heath

Wading through trees,
my feet tread down branches
to the ground.
Unseen holes threaten
as the ground gives way
and swaps places with the sky.
Here, where I can almost touch blue above,
my eyes are walking with my feet,
tree walking over unexpected pits and falls,
dark drainage of cold air,
earthly vertigo: one foot
then the other, above the ground.

If only

I could bring a forest home
I'd have the chance to live within its bounds.
Great branches writing on the sky would roam
And write their whispered spell upon these grounds.
I yearn always for rustling leaves a-flight
And ageless branches hung on thick barked trunks
I yearn for mossy hugs midst branches tight,
The promise of an enclave quiet as monks.
In winter's emptiness I hear their call,
In spring they sing the flourishing of life.
In autumn their wild colours clothe my soul
And summer's shady green is balm for strife.
A grove of trees counts just as much as friends
For in their reach life's circle never ends.

Airport

Five hundred years
is folded, compressed, rivetted,
tempered and moulded
into metal geometry.
Tons of feather weight like the flash
of a sword through the air,
planes are unleashed.
Triangles, nosed in, focus harnessed
poised direction on the verge, on the brink,
on the cusp of the horizon,
on Leonardo's intake of breath.

Sergeant Duncan Carseldine, POW, knits himself a jumper using fencing wire for needles

Pinky brown, woollen textured furrow:
Knit one, purl one, pass the wool between,
Plaited cables from these wires farrow.

Away from home the wool soaks up my sorrow,
The cuffs are subtle army khaki green,
Pinky brown, woollen textured furrow.

Random wools of beg and steal and borrow:
Not a combination that I've ever seen,
Plaited cables from these wires farrow.

Concentration leaves less time to wallow:
Homely witness to everything that's been,
Pinky brown, woollen textured furrow.

Memories from home cause me to swallow:
Luckily, I've slimmed right down to lean,
Plaited cables from these wires farrow

My jumper holds a promise for tomorrow,
A jumper made for Sergeant Carseldine:
Pinky brown, woollen textured furrow,
Plaited cables from these wires farrow.

Postcard: I am in good spirits and good health.

Australian War Memorial

When the guns are quiet and hate has been dusted
The tanks and trucks are cleaned
The artifacts arranged and labelled,
The medals glitter on their plaques,
Steel helmets, frilled, drilled, corroded and
eroded by time, sit silent,
the remains of a Hudson aircraft engine
unfurls like a metal posy or wreath.

Reflective glass, hourly shows and the café take over.
The ink sketches become sleight of hand,
The watercolours on paper ghostly,
Clothing, blankets and quilts, with
embroidered scars, flower,
Cable laying in a jungle clearing at Gemas gleams
through fragile sun's rays.

Scraps are framed,
The lions of Menin Gate are repaired
and bare their teeth in an enigmatic smile.
Fields of crosses are mute, with artificial shadows,
and the sudden fugitive glimpse
of a tender, arched, exposed and vulnerable
human neck speaks the same language
as valour, honour and waste.

When you are a teacher

the world is new every day.
Yesterday's trials have receded
until you have Samuel again
egging them all on until you break,
resolve weakened like old elastic.
Who are you reining in?
Yourself,
with your artful phenomenological questioning,
your New Age Socratic method.
Nothing has changed.
Just tell us what you want, they chorus,
and is it going to be assessed.
And here you are
with your tabula rasa,
the joy of learning undimmed,
but fundamentally uncommunicable.
The reality is they have to find it
for themselves
and so many won't.
so much is wasted:
teaching, a guilty nomenclature,
a fragile grammar of hope,
a genetically modified hyperlink
of trust.

Weston I

Sitting on the hill, my hands cup an imaginary coffee.
Lilac and mauve blur on the crema
while I feel the sun's glow on my back.
The horizon is still, cold and pale. The coffee perfects the view.
The morning thaws and suburban crystals project
as everyday fractals jostle and compete, reflecting,
refracting their neighbours' desires, wishes and dreams.
The reality is concrete enough.
Spaces are claimed.
Trees, such as they are, stand slimly vertical,
sucking in their sides to appear svelte and sexy
like their owners.
Roof surveys roof.
Grey deflects grey, deflects black.
Rear-vision checks for rifts in status, temperament and influence.
Porticos and visors fail as unremitting glare of observation
overpowers the need for shade.
The hills sing softly in the background,
an old tune, vaguely familiar.

Weston II

Above the new Sikh temple, the roof is a V
pointing downwards, inwards
like an arrow to the earth.
Around it, the new suburb spreads,
rows of boxes, containers and piles of cubes
stacks of rooms, facing north.
A lake rests between, reflecting the sky above.
The houses suck in the air
through their mouths, which are otherwise silent.
Arteries pulse alongside –
hopes, fears, intentions, desires, wishes,
regrets, barrelling along towards their own horizons.
The hearts are in the houses
The spirit is in the air
The water lies on the ground
The arrow strikes the earth.
Icarus has fallen, just this side of the hills
In the distance.
Flames leap and the fire engine races past.

It finally rained today

after an odyssey of clouds
rampaged and fulminated
In that parallel universe, the sky.
I looked for a Greek god,
a link to a culture of water and words
and found forty nine, not counting
the three in ones, Sirens, the Gorgons, The Graeae,
Or Σέργιο, God of the Frogs and currents, whirlpools,
amphibians, all linked to rivers and oceans and
not the simple blessing I sought in that sheet of silver.

I run as the drops wet my back
I watch the overflowing gutters
as the water shivers the window.
Long awaited
and beyond cliché
an ocean of sky
lapping a tumult of air and light.
Wonder as water, spirit with weight,
water as wonder, body of light.
Relief, wordless thanks, the mind mere air,
and it is dissolved and gone again.
Three in one, I am grateful.

Oakey Hill Electricity Substation

Electricity is harnessed like a forest of fuel rods,
wrinkled charges pressured into dangerous cores,
grey pencil posts waiting in their wired enclosure
to be discharged.
Cars power past.
A magpie's song curves musically off grid.
Giants tension steel muscles and triangulate.
Humming staves soar into the horizon like steel hills and valleys,
The breeze riffles the air and moves on.
There are trilobites, resting,
their energy conserved against time and its flow,
stockpiled like my thoughts, still,
the way a lance needles to a point to prick the air
even when released without a target, too soon,
or wide of the mark.
Stockpiled like my words, compressed, distilled,
before they uncurl and surge.

The National Museum

Framed by oblique ribs of the museum café
I survey the view,
knife chopping surface of the lake in a severe wind
through needle leaves of the pine to my left
and its rose gold, coruscating armour.
Across the lake the water jet sweeps sideways rain.
It has been that kind of week.
The National Library sits imperturbably by.
Nothing about received knowledge is elastic,
it merely endures.
A family has taken their noisy offspring outside
for morning tea
where the noise rivals the cold in its intensity.
No one is at the lakeside gym. All is grey.
A young man nearby rages, rattling the bars of
his wordless cage and we look on helplessly.
A Korean woman at my table burbles like a stream
as her vowels ripple over and around the china.
I have come by myself.
The couple on my right have been to the Cartier show –
huge crystals, refractions beyond compare, glitter
that is missing on the lake today.
Framed by the architecture of my choc cherry
bread and butter pudding
I survey the view.
My daughter never wants to see me again.
I survey the view.
I eat my cake.

Northbourne Avenue reborn

Avenue of trees dishevelled
dappled shade meanly unravelled
Burley Griffin's plan untrammelled

Trees are sadly now all levelled
naked jewel, glaring, frazzled
Canberra, planning jewel unrivalled.

Civic sparkle, purses shrivelled
more choices for the road less travelled
Burley Griffin's plan untrammelled
Canberra, planning jewel unrivalled.

Autumn Elegy

For Brian

It is the leaning in of autumn.
Long shadows reach tenderly
along sunny grass that does
not want to yield just yet.
It is always too soon.
A golden glow hangs in the air,
A bird flies past, low and light.
I see leaves flutter and
I recall you dancing
your shadow tenderly embracing
the air
reaching out to others who
extend their arms mutely in return,
in gold,
in shadow.
You lean in,
Did you mean to let go?
Too soon, not yet.
Not yet.

Yesterday

winter arrived.
Drawing in its breath, winter stillness
lay down overnight in the garden
under a silver cover, while I was asleep.
Behind my security door,
I was tucked in,
under two beautiful green blankets
edged in green satin,
a summer border
for my dreams.

Breaching my defences
in the morning, the sun lured me out,
and I remembered why I love winter:
the crisp clear wintry air
sparkles all the way down.
Woolly comfort, rugging up,
the way your hands warm up
after you've felt them freezing,
and everything glows.
And when it's grey and raining,
and the wind whistles,
and it's warm inside afterwards,
a hot drink is wonderful,
a fire works its familiar magic,
a book beckons,
a lamp glows,
and the electric blanket is on.

Billboard Boasting

My house is me and I am it.
I inhabit this skin at the same time as I select it from the cupboard
and go out and reveal myself in my wardrobe of well-worn selves.
I hang it up in the cupboard at night and go out in my dreams.
I have the seemingly unattainable right within arm's reach,
the pace, passion and proximity of transformable experience, at
home.
I don't have to buy it in Civic; I don't have to find it in a
night club
or on a billboard.
It is here at home, a three-bedroom ex-govy,
with the ghosts of families
who made the banal uniquely their own
and who had nothing in particular
to prove.
Hipping and thighing*
around the garden
I wonder if Persephone
was a size 16 or greater.
Was she relieved to hide
in the dark season
to reduce before the spring?
Blushing cheeks are all very well
but beauty's flesh belies
dark Nature's rage
below the world.
All flowers are new:
The bulb is the mysterious
'what lies beneath'
and that's where it stays.

* 'hipping and thighing' – Clive James

A cry of witnesses

is as nothing in the back row
of the chorus of progress.
No one grieves the loss
of a pre-owned empty shell,
the dead pledge of the past.
Spilt milk, disappointment,
or simple, outdated,
run-down content. It is all of a piece.
A new oyster is the promise of a new oyster
beyond gilt-edged mortgage rime and rim.
Celebrate the pearl of great price again:
You can live the dream,
permanently in love,
an eternal bouquet open
where youth and freedom feed endlessly
off each other
in the eternal mirror
of desire.

Autumn

I caught you this morning and it was 7.28
because I looked down at my watch
and it was over in a few seconds,
Autumn's fingertip on the tree branch,
a single phrase of light,
like the first chord of a song I know comes next,
like the breeze when it lets its guard down,
resting on the branch and its colour shows,
the heart of summer weighed against a feather
the warmth of gold weighted against a leaf,
like the rustle of an angel's skirt
out of the corner of my eye
or the way the air closes after the flicker of a wing,
I felt its gold rapture rupture,
wonder wander
and then I packed my lunch
and went off to work.

Gardeners

enjoy control beneath the sun.
It's one decision after another – you can stay,
but you must go.
The rustle of Nature's passing, the flutter of her hem,
the wisp of her breath, slips past the corner of my hopes,
in a parallel universe where goddesses wander,
grass always green under their feet
and no weeds.
I too, survey my kingdom.
I gaze into the morning pinkness where anemones flutter
taller than me,
and offer their wind flowers to the sky.
I gaze into the afternoon gold where apricot dahlias
taller than me,
dance their sunset coronas with the sky.
I gaze into the green of time where the golden elm,
taller than me,
lavishes chartreuse upon heaven's veil.
They may have done it all without me.
I yank out a huge euphorbia,
smaller than me,
up to the sky and down to the ground.
I am the Queen here.

Canberra

A parcel of Prime Ministers
A pandemic of Prime Ministers
A pandora of Prime Ministers
A platform of Prime Ministers
A parchment of Prime Ministers
A promise of Prime Ministers

Contours are taken
Containment lines are traced
The circuitry untangled
Suburbs are mapped and proofed
Pockets are deepened

So much rustling, crackling, tweaking
Crinkling and crumpling,
Brown paper inflections
Flurry of postmen,
paper planes,
Nudging and jostling,
Creases and winks,
Smiles and whiskers,
And so it begins
An eternal a.m. of p.ms.

Capital Hill trepanned

A steel halo is welded to the capital,
a sturdy sculpture to have and to hold
the dome of the nation, conduct lightning safely
beneath the crown of heaven.
Foundations are buried deep in the rock of ages,
in God we used to trust,
a subtle grip upon back to back boomerangs,
flying scissors in this no longer Terra nullius.
A warren, a hive, a colony of drones,
infernal passageways of intentions,
best hopes lost,
a bunker of compromise,
the last den of the cockroach.

Bunnings I

Our Lady of Succour resides at Bunnings.
She is accompanied by Saint Antony,
Patron Saint of lost things. Theirs is
a joint tenancy of beneficence and bounty.

Their presence beams,
materials from first principles, a radiant
interior exterior Estapol gleam
suspended in the heavenly vacuum
above the aisles marked 1 to 24 and beyond.

All who come receive their smiling
reassurance, redemption with no hidden markup,
no competitive edge.
What you see is what you will receive,
with a barcoded blessing
at the end of every wanded exit.

Their holy day is Saturday,
when the Host is handed out to those
who present themselves, newly washed
with hope and licked with promise.

Bunnings retails potential
which is never vanquished.
All failures are forgiven
and forgotten.
An idea is renewed with possibility,
the future dusted with dreams
and bright imaginings.

Down every aisle handles reach out
to be seized. Red-coated attendants
are there to serve and women are indulged,
as they reach out to touch
the hem of their garments.

If Mum can do it,
there is more hope for Dad
who is not a handyman at all
and may have been rejected
by failure's fickle friendship.

Bunnings is open early
for anticipation and preparation
of the day's labour.
It is open late for the regretful
and the over-committed.
No one is turned away.
Everyone is an equal
before the Lord of all Creation.

Bunnings II

No need to steal, to covet or to poach.
transports of delight across the seas lap and laminate.
Quality Time is available for purchase,
not merely branded, glued and laid,
but bonded, spanned and spelled.

A floating floor in all its mystery can be your passage
whether it is Ancient Cypress, Russet Olive, Vintage Allspice,
Diamond Gloss Linen Wood or Cherry,
you can walk through history every day.
Sherwood Oak on sale, Luminous,
Dark Misty, Moonshadow Suede,
Autumn Antique, wild and smoked.

For the convicted, new world Walnut
and Diamond Blackbutt Ironbark
and Tasmanian Blackwood,
Sydney Blue and Northern Rivers Gum,
Berrima Ash are splayed.

Choose your path. Sound Logic hushes your steps
with soft silent steamed Patchwork
Cappuccino by the metre.
Dressed and undressed,
wood circles the years with truth.
Walking on the forest floor
treads lightly upon the earth.
A ticket of leave for today's currency lads and lasses
building a deck at Bunnings.
Cross your floor. Cross my heart.

Bunnings III

Picnics and barbecues are
temporarily stilled.
Outdoor meals have moved indoors.

Lounges, gazebos, plastic chairs,
netted, woven and slung,
umbrellas, summer clouds gazetted and taut,
stretched for two, for four, for
families and friends,
are waiting.

Inca barbecues, Olmec clay,
Jumbuck chimneys with fire poker
included, compete,
with Rustic Fire Pits, Venetian Braziers and
the Laser-cut Metal Fire Box
in their passionate promises.

Meanwhile,
a glass table frosts over
and winter warps cane chairs.

On Lake Tuggeranong

orange blades scissor the wind.
A half moon hangs sliced above our
hemisphere of blue.

It is ten past two, too, to, as time
sweeps on and the minute hand races
the hour for a head start.
Like municipal semaphore, waving,
indicating an axis of return,
encroaching clash of past and future,
an arrow pointed down but open in reverse.

Like wind arms generating power
this arc cuts time into slices of pie
for your enjoyment.

Sometimes it is still but this is merely
the orange pausing inside its skin
before the peel is endlessly breached,
yet entire. It is a Canberra dervish,
a new angle on mystic potential, physics,
or hurdygurdy money go round
against the horizon.

At the Portrait Gallery

Feather and the Goddess Pool

Feather is known for her youthful and vibrant character.
Her skin is like the surface of the sea,
wrinkling back on itself, over and under, blurring.
Her stomach is a sucking pool,
a vortex of uncompromising years.
Her body is speaking its own language.
Life has tattooed her in ruthless lines
with a crude stylus.
Her arms splay her working hide, her leather coat.
She stands on the shore of her sister, the sea.
Like the feather around her neck, steel or bone,
She waits on time,
And she can fly.

Civic Plaza

A pack of wild dogs
In forward lurch,
Bandages flying,
Springs through the Civic Plaza,
Metal scrounging for metal.
In the distance, a nubile, pink, princess girlie
Leans out towards them,
Flowers trailing,
Plastic puppies by her side.

It will be messy.
The dogs know no master
And the girlie is not yet
Bridled by experience.
Several bird people look on, detached,
And a nearby sheep lounges in an armchair,
Feet up, all care gone. It's all about spectacle,
One fantasy after another.

Clear Complexions

A crepe myrtle has skin, and skin tone,
taut and smooth and firm to the touch.
Crepe is in the flower, not the skin.
Although bark flakes off,
time's blush delineates perfection.

The Angophora dwarfs the crepe myrtle.
It insinuates bulk into the sky.
Its trunks are larger. Slim is not appropriate.
Sturdy, curvy, wavy, tall, limber, with elbows.
And their crowning glory?
Wrinkles and dimples.
Wrinkles and dimples.

Eric Thake, War Artist, Noemfoor Island, 1945

In a broken shaving mirror nailed to a tree,
A crack severs half my face,
A single eye represents one half of me,
My spirit fractured in this surreal place.

A crack severs half my face:
I look behind me, scene fragmented,
My spirit fractured in this surreal place,
The sky is broken and the world demented.

I look behind me, scene fragmented:
Another figure broken on a tree.
The sky is broken and the world demented,
Compassion scatters, every word a plea.

Another figure broken on a tree
Distant, isolated, no longer one of us
Compassion scatters, every word a plea,
A silent death, appalling lack of fuss.

Distant, isolated, no longer one of us,
A single eye represents one half of me.
Lives splinter, crack and shiver in the glass,
A broken shaving mirror nailed to a tree.

Grave Dimensions

> Two Marys
> Maggiore   Minore
> Mary   Marija
> Mere Mary   Mary mia

Like a Viking grave ship,
                Floating on a pile of rubble,
A stone vessel, poised to slip its mooring,
                Concrete icebergs,
Ave Maris Stella.   Flotsam and jetsam of stones,
Grave offerings, garnished in glory,
                Clumps of earth, bleached
Riot in pink; spring wishes with sails set,
                And buffeted by the weather,
Petals puffed with kisses,
                Earthy froth and gravel bubble.
Silk caresses. Buoyant blooms
                Steel mesh arcs, tangled
Dusted with dew, bud
                Latitude and longitude above the waves.
In an eternal spring.
                Grave goods,
Escorted by Jesus himself, in triplicate,
                Platform and headstone, teeter alone
Foreground, middle ground and background,
                Above a tumultuous tumulus,
A focused Trinity, infinity,
                A tsunami on its path to oblivion,

Vases, urns and jugs, proud sentinels of love.
                A wave on a featureless ocean
Still texting Heaven
                Of somebody's love.
On Social media. A silent line in the records.

Nearby,   unnamed babies,   marked by slivers of stone   lie in the grass.

Stillborn?   Born, still?   Born.   Still.

Storm in the Outback
At the National Gallery

When the storm breaks
it slashes spears, sticks and slicing
diagonal thrusts.

The cloud fills the sky,
a black and sharp-edged rectangle
of intention.

Charcoal bleeds, milk ribbons
ochre rivulets
and rusty slurries.

Criss crossed, colliding, transecting
the void, they grid, grade and grille
the air

Primeval geometry is not round.
Beyond the curve is straight energy
Pure lines of light,
And the ever extended plain of dark.

Ngalyod the Rainbow Serpent

Hands by her side, whole and entire
Eve never had to face this.
Upside down, suspended
in the gut of the serpent
coiled three times around,
its head over its shoulder,
tongue flicking two eyes together
in the night.
In the black hole;
Dots dance before her eyes,
splinters align,
thoughts stream plasma
as she is absorbed
into the infinite geometry
of the curve.

Ngayunangalku

The Spirit Being of Lake Disappointment
Stands like drift wood,
His insignificant grain
Overwritten, scratched,
Inscribed with hungry needle prickings.
Smooth, no splinters or hair shirt,
No rough edges,
Just a few shadows,
Especially below the nose
Where a triangle points the chin
And fangs the eyeless outlook above.
Breathed out, whisper thin,
His claws in parched pockets
Hold nothing
And already his legs are
knuckled, bent and bowed
Before the future.

At the Portrait Gallery

Joel

I see him lying there, suspended,
Underneath the empty tray
Of a semi-trailer, in the shade
On the spare tyre
Chained beneath the metal plate.

His arm falls to the ground,
A fluid line of gravity
Pointing down the years
Since the Renaissance painting
Where I have seen it before.
The glare and the stillness
White out the town
Except for this illegitimate shade.

A teenage pieta,
Impassive, still and unwavering
Wisp of vulnerability,
Chest bones arched, stomach flat.
A fallen angel? Or simply
A statement of teenage disenchantment
In a sunburnt outback town,
Where culture has no future
And being gay will see him
Run over by a steady roll
Of trucks such as this,
Tray empty, bleached in the sun.

George Lambert, Self-portrait with Gladioli

No one can deny that I have a presence.
A self-portrait that looks like someone else did it
must surely tell you that I have this certain something.
It's not the velvet dressing gown that does it,
though I have to say,
the sheen on my wide shoulders and slim waist
speak subtly of manliness.
My pipe rests between my teeth, although,
truth to tell, I am biting hard,
concentrating on looking casual yet sophisticated.
My huge hands are itching to articulate the air,
the textures I enjoy.
My forehead is distinguished,
as I have a good head of hair and am aging well.
The gladioli are a conceit, perhaps,
but a floral tribute always goes down well.
My only concern, no, mild anxiety,
is that my head looks too small.

Parliament House Democracy. Closed for Refurbishment

Justice may be blind
but Democracy wears dark glasses and has a headache.
It is a case of all in, few holds barred,
or is it all holds bared
so we can see every sorry blunder
every blunder sorry'd,
the bloodshot bleariness
of tired and a bit stressed,
overwrought, overdone and undone
late at night, on Twitter, through darkened branches.

The mechanics of oversight and insight
have been reduced to mere windows
where double glazing still needs to be replaced
and the light from above is not the same
as the light within.
The sky's the limit, but thick white cataracts
obscure the view out and in.

Liberality of spirit is reduced
to a slimline necktie in blue,
squalls between members swell, all at sea;
Beyond Blue is a measure of despair.
Propriety is sold at auction
and Value is a unit of currency for the highest bidder.

Parliament Hill is like a site not found,
an iceberg broken from the main shelf
a nameless carton boxed and wrapped for storage
a lump of sugar, cubed, and crystallised for later,
the same view from all sides;
a whiteout before our eyes,
a no-man's-land in 3D,
a Christo knock-off
or a Rachel Whiteread plaster cast
of the mental space within;
a Parthenon full of loose marbles
rattling around, glassy irises with the lights out.

The entire building was covered in white tarpaulins for window upgrade.

The Tram

In front of my nose,
the approaching horizon
is coming into view just over my knees
at about waist height,
sneaking under the elbows
until I am more forwards than backwards
and all the possibility of tomorrow is here now.
A snout has all the doglike promise
of adventure in the everyday.
The tram unwinds the thread of the labyrinth,
there and back.

The frost

crystallises at ankle level,
fog breathes slowly in and out,
a silver murmur made visible.
Lungs like open palms clench in the cold.
Sharp air too delicate to hold
cripples the fingers to the touch.
Autumn has stilled,
the leaves have fallen and settled,
little papery crusts of summer from the skin of the world.

The leaf blower hurls its voice,
invisible fuel wreathes around the ankles in a noxious swirl
the noise argues with the air
and scabs the morning.

Outreaches

There may be no spire pointing skywards
but there is an aerial, a wireless needle nudging the cloud,
a channel to infinite data storage for upload and download
and Golden Arches signal the drive-through for goodness,
the pickle of remorse and beefy blessings' juices.
Apartments align like pews
and there is sanctuary in the landscape's far enfolding hills,
mantled with an innocence of snow, briefly unsullied,
a perfect horizon.
Nevertheless, the western sun will scald Regulus again,
eyelids stitched open, watching real estate redemption
as value becomes the end in itself.
If angels sing overhead, windows are double glazed
against the unremitting glare and dazzle of Heaven
and a monotone hum accompanies the icy wind.
The map is now the territory and
Home Sweet Home is reproduced entire,
For ever and ever,
Amen.

www.ingramcontent.com/pod-product-compliance
Lightning Source LLC
Chambersburg PA
CBHW072136070526
44585CB00016B/1708